Dropping the Eyelids

Nonfiction for the Soul

Ernest Dempsey

Modern History Press

Ann Arbor, MI

Learn more at www.ErnestDempsey.com

ISBN: 978-1-61599-631-5

Published by
Modern History Press
5145 Pontiac Trail
Ann Arbor, MI 48105

www.ModernHistoryPress.com
info@ModernHistoryPress.com

Tollfree 888-761-6268 (USA/CAN/PR)
Fax 734-663-6861

Contents

To The Sun

The one that gives us life, and lights it for us

Preface

Writing nonfiction, to me, is always an act of returning to oneself. It's the time when I become *me* and my voice goes out to the world straight from me, not via another character employed as my envoy. Yet, my voice resonates via all the entities and the void that make the narrative. I fill these things, places, people, and air with my voice. It's the echo of me that tells the story, delivers the message, and returns to me.

In putting together this book, I literally returned to myself. Though these essays span over 15 years of my writing life, most were written within the last six years. The idea for putting together a book of nonfiction, however, came fairly recently. The practice of regularly penning down a set of nonfiction essays started with my creative nonfiction course that I took at the Portland Community College, Oregon, in winter 2014. A few months ago, as I was going through the writing assignments of that folder, the muse fired that flame at me, one that makes writers what they are. I wrote some new essays as they came to me, here in Orlando, FL, with the motivation to create enough to put together a short book. Finally, I threw in a few older essays and edited or re-wrote some to vibrate with the prevailing mood and spirit of writing.

The return to my voice as me, instead of lending it out to fictional characters, necessitated that certain names and identifying characteristics be changed to protect the privacy of real-life people mentioned in some of these essays. Individual writings vary in themes and accordingly the narration, but I suppose the general feel of these pieces tends to shift to the darker side. I prefer, however, not to preset the reader's reception by getting the author out there before the book.

I thank you all for taking the time to read these essays. Do share your comments, thoughts, and/or questions. I'll try to respond via editor@ernestdempsey.com.

Ernest Dempsey

December 05, 2021

Apology to Old Companions

Sitting in Portland, Oregon, past midnight, sipping coffee, I write these lines to you all who kept me good company in my years of difficult times in Pakistan. I remember having just a few hours of steady power supply and internet connection back there; but all the time having your company for pleasure. The moment I needed you, I always found you ready for a silent embrace. Such was our sweet bond. Your faces on paper—what appeared to be an arrangement of letters—served as a cordial when everything else was falling apart: the terror-struck land, the dry and rough weather, terrifying levels of pollution, and above all, those attitudes and utterances I hardly want to remember.

Yet I chose to leave you. I flew to a country with many dear friends waiting to welcome me. And I had to leave you as papers filled with ink, in my hand, caged inside closets in two rooms in different houses. Worse, I didn't even say to you I was sorry to leave you behind while hugging all my family before departing. Maybe there never was any distance between us, one that defines most human relationships. With you, I was always so very *one* that I never felt we were separate, or could be separated. The smell of the closet, the layer of dust, and sometimes a spider's newly woven web over some of you, all gave you all a life of your own. I saw in that closet not a pile of notebooks and journals, but an echo of my spirit, my passion, and my happiness. Should I apologize to you then, for leaving myself there in your form? Won't it imply just apologizing to myself?

I'll let you be the judge. How you will let me know of your ruling is your work. Remember how you made your own life—by impregnating my mind with your existence, then moving my blood toward the pen to carve you in physical form? You had the power of making me create; I would not be surprised should you find your own way to connect with me across the ocean. If that didn't happen, I would be glad to offer an apology, which in itself would not be a happy moment. However, I choose to put more faith in you than the world puts in its idols.

For now, I am leaving the question of apology open. Time will unite us again, probably on your calling. Here in Portland, I enjoy coffee and connect with you in the same way I did in Hangu while drinking hot tea and interacting with you, late into the night. There, we said "good night" to each other without speaking a word, in a silent but constant rhythm of music played by our friendship. Here, we will meet again someday, say in Hollywood, probably having lunch with a celebrity; and when the celebrity takes a break to speak to media, perhaps I'll come up with something that amounts to an apology; and I am sure you'll help me find the right words, as you always do.

Backyard Beauty

"I'll see if there's a rose in my backyard so I could harvest it." The young man's message set the pro-lifer in me on instant red alert. I learnt a bit late that the short film challenge posted by the organizer required making a rose a part of the film in some way. My script, sent to my young director, didn't include a rose. I had to think a little about how to word my concern.

"About the rose, how about we use an artificial one instead of plucking the rose in your backyard?" I asked as I wrote him back. He was, as I expected, curious to know why. So I had to explain.

"I happen to be pro-life, which means not only am I a vegetarian because of my advocacy for animal rights but generally against waste or abuse of nature and part of that is abstaining from unnecessary killing of plant life as well. Sorry if it sounds like radical environmentalism. But I'll be glad if you understand and respect my request." I was glad to see he agreed though he did say that he felt my approach was a bit extreme.

Next came his turn as he read my full script for possible revision.

"As a churchgoer Christian," he wrote, "I won't like to work with a line that has both the name Jesus and a swear word in it. I'll need to edit out the swear word." On an average day, the radical writer in me hates to let any editorial clippers trim my lines. But with my heart so romantically fixated on that backyard beauty, the one I'd never seen and was likely never going to see, I sent him a nod.

Life happened to us both and we ended up not making that short film together. The challenge deadline had long expired when I eventually teamed up with my artist friend Annie in Houston, after returning to America, and made the film without any rose. I, however, continue to think of that rose sometimes. How long did it get to live in the young filmmaker's backyard? Long enough I hope to feed many bees and create many other roses via their wanderings. Who knows one of these days, if I am taking a walk around the neighborhood in Orlando, I see a rose, close to a fence, looking my way and saying in its backyard beauty language, "Been waiting for you here."

Breaking the Cage

You and I are one. You have wings; I don't. Yet we become one as your wings will bring you to the cage that holds me. Once you fall in here, your captor will cage you separately, given how small you happen to be and also own those wings that you can use anytime to fly away. You are way more free. So you'll get a far more restricting cage—four walls of metal with a tiny door that locks behind you.

Soon as you realize you have been imprisoned, you'll frantically fly about within the cage, crashing your soft wings against the iron bars. You can't get out. You'll scream for help. No one listens, not what you are saying. They'll just give you a little food, a little water, and return to their chores. For hours, you'll struggle to break the cage. You don't want to eat, or drink water, or rest in a prison. You never thought you'd be in such a prison one day, your world reduced from the universe to an inch of it in no time. No, you don't want to live like this, held enslaved in this cage. Your heart knows it'll stop beating in mourning what you lost. Helpless, exhausted, starving, you'll drop dead in your cage. Your captor will have a moment of frustration for losing you so quickly. Your dead body will be thrown out because now it looks bad in the cage and can attract bugs.

I'll mourn you. I'll quietly mourn your death—the death of your body through which you acted out the anguish of your soul. I won't see that distress anymore. You broke the cage. You flew away without your wings and got way up there, far beyond the reach of any captors. Can you spot me from up there? Can you see me more miserable in my cage—

one that has no walls, and no door? Your freedom does set me free somehow. I know this because you and I are one.

Concert Thanatos

Two decades ago, when shingles erupted on my body one summer, I witnessed a new kind of music. It didn't have sound but played its tune via feeling. Each neural firing generating from my chest shot through me with a pang, creating a rhythm of pain. More than a decade later, a similar tune would play itself from my chipped tooth in Portland, Oregon. Different place, different time, somewhat different rhythm, but nearly the same melody, and greater loudness.

The tunes kept playing on my body at intervals chosen solely by the player. Four years ago, it struck two notes at once in my chest as I got bruised ribs from a sudden bout of bronchitis. The symphony screamed from the ribcage every time I breathed, coughed, or sneezed—its loudness increasing accordingly. Even changing sides and getting out of the bed brought echoes of the symphony.

Over a year later, one winter afternoon, my upper back suddenly got *musical* after I ran outside, without enough padding against the chilly wind, to check on the pet dog, Dumbo. I agreed to let a topical analgesic rubbed on my back to quell the cacophony. A surprise event for sure, yet far from being the last.

One overcast afternoon, after my return to Florida, my friends and I visited Blue Springs. Swimming in cool water, at a safe distance from the gators, was fun, until it was time to get out of the water. Then I heard something bump into the bottom of the ramp under the water. Within a second, my left foot declared itself as the *something* by playing the

Ruin Your Day tune. Out on the ramp, where I struggled to keep a normal face, I saw my foot bloody near the toe. Thanks to the sanitized wipes we carried with us, the scary red part was quickly covered, or I could imagine my ears bursting with the sinister tune played as if on steroids.

The body will keep playing the organ for the Thanatos concert each time pain lays its hands on it. Then comes the day of the last symphony. The music stops, and the organ is discarded.

Dark Cloud Tune

The moment I stepped onto the grass in the front yard, a sudden, intense pain shot up through me from my right foot. Uttering a muffled cry of pain, I lifted my foot above the ground to look at it. A sharp bone fragment had penetrated my rubber sneaker all the way, running straight inside the ball of my foot. Instinct moved my hand electrically and as I pulled the culprit out, dropping my shoe, fresh red blood gushed out of the wound. Pressing on it with my fingers, I limped back on one foot to the cemented floor, calling my brother's name aloud to come outside and help me. The next week would see my foot anointed and bandaged, and myself limping to the bathroom whenever nature called. It was hard to believe that within ten minutes of entering home—after a sleepless night at the Muscat Airport, loss of my wallet during the travel, and a five-hour back-breaking road trip from the airport to my hometown in a stone-age van—I got stabbed in the foot before even saying hello to my mom. Sitting on the floor as my brother bandaged my foot and my mom and siblings watched, I was resisting the urge to look up at the sky. I didn't want to see any dark cloud up there, looking down my way with a belittling smile.

~ ~ ~

When I got the US visa, finally after two-and-a-half years of administrative processing by the authorities, I heaved a long-held sigh of relief. Two years that psychologically brought me to my knees would at last be put to rest. The recent month-long trip to Nepal had given me a break, a desperately needed one, but then the wifi didn't work in the hotels I got there, costing me half of the month's payment for the missed work. The mystical white clouds and enchanting morning mist of mountainous Nepal did play their healing role in getting my spirit back on its feet. Now with the US visa in my folder, I could return to America and live the peaceful days just like the three-and-a-half years spent there previously. Admittedly, had I known that my US visa was coming in October, I wouldn't have visited Nepal in desperation in August to get a break from my misery. I would rather have saved the $1500 for my US trip. Had the dark cloud been at play here too? Was it behind the American embassy's policy of not providing any info on the expected time of issuance of one's visa?

With active resistance to belief in the supernatural and a claim to adherence to science, the last thing I wanted was the acceptance of a dark cloud haunting me as fact. A happy return to America was going to put that supernatural dark cloud to rest forever.

~ ~ ~

I feared I'd miss my connecting flight from Virginia's Dulles Airport to Orlando since the weather caused a delayed departure from London Heathrow, and then the plane kept hovering over Dulles, waiting for clearance to land. The familiar dark cloud tune had started thrumming on my nerves, despite the excitement of liberation steering the mood. Eventually the plane landed and by the time I went through immigration, the connecting flight to Orlando had left—the last flight from Dulles to Orlando that evening. But so what? I was back in America and was given six months to stay, the maximum a visitor gets on any single trip. I searched the nearby hotels online and tried to book one. It didn't work. So I got a cab and walked into one. A Hispanic woman who had difficulty understanding and speaking

English told me coldly that I couldn't get a room without online booking. Damn! Good thing I had the cab waiting. I returned to Dulles Airport. I had to spend the rest of the night there and catch the first morning flight to Orlando. As I waited for my flight, pacing the terminal, struggling to shoo away sleep, the dark cloud tune raged in crescendos on my nerves. I looked across the glass door to the entrance. The snowflakes in the air outside danced to the Christmas music playing inside the airport. It started toning down the dark cloud tune. Calm started settling on my mind. *Yes, it's goanna be all good. All good after this one last stretch of insanity. Tomorrow's gonna start a new chapter.* I started dreaming with open eyes while my eyelids kept getting heavier.

~ ~ ~

Life was falling back in place in Orlando. Reunion with friends and a few trips to places of interest reclaimed an assurance to normalcy. The trips I looked most forward to, however, were coming up in spring after weather would go mellow on the west coast. The spring did arrive, but preceding it came the least expected—a sudden shutting down of the world as those who rule it declared a "pandemic." My disbelief in the nature and scale of this phenomenon didn't prevent the airlines from cancelling my trips. The imposition of muzzling oneself with a face covering for "everyone's safety" was enough to kill my spirit of travel and reunion with friends in other states. Weeks of this global scare stretched out into months. The dark cloud tune, loud and constant, played inside out of me. I had to file for an extension of stay amidst the international travel restrictions and was told to wait in the country until they decide on my application.

Five months down the road, I await the decision on my application, spending every dollar carefully while already in debt. I go out daily into the backyard to get fresh air. My eyes scan the sky for clouds, apprehensively looking for the one that has clubbed down the optimist in me. Both hope and fear sit on my sight as I look at the clouds. Perhaps I hope to let it know via looking straight at it that I've accepted my surrender. And I fear that it'll still look down on me with a belittling smile, leaving me seething to its haunting tune.

Dropping the Eyelids

The current is noisy and its uproar sounds so fierce, it's intimidating. Looking at it makes me at once scared and challenged. One step ahead, and it can easily yank me off my feet, taking me for a ride I'm not sure I'm ready to take. Yes, I know what direction I'm heading, for there is but just one. I won't have much say in choosing my destination. But I am certain to be carried where the current is set to reach.

The valley down there is green and promising. There are quite a few bends along the channel of the stream and where it slows down—way down there—minimal effort can get me off the raging fury of the current and onto the valley. The cuts and bruises I get during the course of the ride will hurt at first. But I've heard that one gets used to them sooner or later, depending on how you chose to take the ride. There are those who fling themselves into the current in excitement and have been known to land safely at any of the turns down there without showing any serious injuries or damage—at least not something readily visible. But I've heard the ones skeptical of the green, visible way down there usually get roughed up in the current before they make it to the land.

What do I have to lose? I ask myself this as I look at the offer the stream has for me: long as I don't try to go against the current, it'll carry me in its volatile flow, its formless arms keeping me safe from other creatures. All I need to do is keep a safe distance from other riders around me. If I can't clearly see it all, the current is said to be kind to those who simply close their eyes whenever something appears intimidating along the way. Just drop my eyelids and I'll end up safe at the valley where others will welcome me to the haven. So I don't have much to lose—nothing, except that dream.

In my dream, I'm in the valley, not the one by the stream, but one with a lake at its center. I stand at the bank looking at the calm blanket of blue spread out in the shape of a circle. On this soft blue stage I see waves dancing in rhythm to the tune of the breeze. They seem like motioning me to join them. My heart beats 'yes' and I go ahead, wading toward the center of the lake. I get there, effortlessly, and though my feet no longer touch the ground, I hold myself up there with minimal effort. The day is bright. I lose sense of time as I play with the never-tiring ballerinas dancing playfully all around me. Then some shadow happens to catch my eye and I realize the sun is on the descent. I feel like I need to see more of this paradise. I look around to see what direction appears best to move.

A state of confusion envelops me from within. There is a green hill on one side of the lake, woods on the other, land with traces of human life ahead, and some island far behind. The different scenes harmoniously transition into one another such that it's difficult to say with confidence where one ends and another begins. I feel there is good waiting to welcome me somewhere there in all those directions. Yet I must choose one, because I have only one body. This intrinsic confinement dictates choice.

No matter which way I choose to go, I must exert to move myself there. There is no certainty as to what I'll find there since those who went there before me have different stories, each woven around their personal quest—some happy, some regretful, and some unsure. I know the sun isn't going to be here for long. So I must choose my direction and start moving before it grows dark. Once it's dark here, I'll be lost. I won't know where I am and what surrounds me. The grounds may be shifting in the dark, the surroundings transforming into creatures coming after me. So I must start moving soon.

What freezes my heart in this warm and pleasing scene is the beauty singing a celebratory note around me, embracing me like I'm its only child. Maybe I can stay the night, thinking of this tune, feeling its constant presence. Maybe I can dream of butterflies dancing over the waves until the light of the day makes the dream come alive. Perhaps I can get this dream promise me safety in the womb of nature until I am ready to move out.

Fighting Big for 'Small'

Not all kids were lazy in leaving their warm, cozy beds on those winter mornings in the hilly town of Hangu in north-west Pakistan. I knew two who were more than ready to jump out of the bed the moment my mom put her slippers on and turned on the light. My younger brother Seth and sister Katie, a few years younger than Seth, were always competing to get to the side of the fireplace where mom made our breakfast—a kettle of tea with bread fried in a little oil in a pan. Both kids were each other's worst enemies at that time of the morning, and the bone of contention was a toast, infamously remembered as 'Small.'

The disputed property in question was actually the slice of bread that lay on top of others in a pack. It was the one that got a little flattened on its upper surface with its corners slightly rounded due to the pressure from the packing. It appeared a bit smaller, like a dwarf of the bread family. Somehow it also became special to Seth and Katie, and both fell madly in love with it. Now each morning, their rivalry over Small translated into a noisy fight that produced more heat in the room than fire from the fireplace and the cloud of angry words exchanged over its possession was far more bitter than the smoke emanating from the fire and the same old frying pan.

Usually waking up a bit late, as I was not in the running for Small, when I entered the room, the war was at its climax with the two warriors screaming at each other and Mother trying to act as the moderator, constantly warning each of them to stop or face consequences. But the fiery proclamations on both sides were unquenchable: "This is mine!" and "You go to hell!" were the exclamations I would hear cross-fired from each side. I believe the entire neighborhood could hear those easily, if they cared.

After living with this scene for some time, my mother started working on possible solutions. Keeping in view that both sides had refused to accept any kind of division of Small, Mother decided whoever got up earlier and sat by the side of the fireplace toward her left would get Small that morning. This created another problem: now both parties intensively started fighting for claiming the preferred seating required to win Small. Worse though, the fight got physical involving pushing and dragging. Mother soon recalled the failed solution and switched to another strategy, namely that Small would go to the two sides alternatively, working by calendar—one day it was Seth who would enjoy rights to Small, and the other day Katie. This worked for some time, but skirmishes kept happening and the two sides often made disputed claims about the calendar, each claiming on the same morning that it was their day to get Small.

Then Mother came up with a more radical but surprisingly more effective solution by which none of the fighting parties got Small; I did. As a punitive measure for the brats, Mother put Small in my plate, and didn't care for the fact that I didn't like Small. It tasted the same but it looked weird and the fact remained that it was smaller in size. To be honest, I never seemed to make sense of why my siblings fought for that piece. However, being the peace-lover that I was, I greeted Mother's decision.

It was a little heartbreaking to see both Seth and Katie giving me those looks like shooting daggers at me while I was eating Small. I didn't offer it to any of them for courtesy, or to honor their love for Small, when both were present in the room. But if one finished earlier or was late in waking up, I silently pushed Small to the other who was there, sitting near me, looking at Small with the eyes of a beggar. And later they would proudly tell each other that they got Small from me. To them, it was a big victory.

If...

I'm in the *if*, for it starts with 'I'. It's not *me*, though. Being *I*, I share the power *if* holds. Yes, the power that is contained in this small word with only two letters. Just as the hydrogen atom with only two fundamental particles is capable of great creation and destruction once the force keeping its natural state of stability is disrupted. Then it becomes something else with an entirely new identity and qualities.

So it is with *if*. It gives me the power to create countless new worlds within minutes. I see a world where my lively friend has graduated from the law school, lives a healthy and happy life with a successful career, supporting his family and helping others in need. This world is just an *if* apart from the one where he died shortly before graduation, stabbed to death by his brother for committing blasphemy. I can see another world lying an *if* away, one where no Hitlers massacred helpless people for their faith or race. In yet another, animals are friends for life, and not only until the truck from the slaughterhouse arrives to take them away.

My curious imagination flashes ahead to catch a glimpse of yet other worlds, gated by other *ifs*. I can see one where, instead of a pen, I'm holding a butcher's knife, stained with thick red, innocent blood. Another world shows me sitting helplessly in a wheelchair in some nursing home, looking wistfully at the birds flying in the open air across the window. Then I see the world where my mother is sitting by a grave, crying; the epitaph on the grave carries my name. I see my older sister sitting by my mother, trying to console her, and unaware of my world where the same grave has the epitaph of her name and a date before my birth. The *intrinsic force* in the *if* overwhelms me. The *I* dissolves back into the here and now. I'm *me* again.

Kid Again

Learning of my cousin's death, the tidings delivered via a Skype message by my brother in Pakistan brought a shock, one that is natural to almost every death news coming from family. I slept poorly and had disturbing dreams that night—dreams that I don't clearly remember. I had made up my mind to call my mom and aunt, my mom's youngest sister, whose 27-year-old son had unexpectedly died of what the doctors believed was an unusual heart attack.

The next day, shock segued into grief as I called my mom's number from my Skype account. When she put my aunt on the phone, I broke down. She asked me how I was doing and sounded composed though I could sense a lifelessness in her voice—maybe my own projected onto hers. But the things I had meant to say to her all vanished. I cried and she heard me and tried to console me.

"Come on son, you are the courageous one," her words felt like creating a title for the state of mind I had suddenly got into—disbelief.

"I just can't believe it's real," I sobbed out. "And I don't have any words. Whatever I thought I'll say to you is gone. I have no words."

"You have said it all," she calmly replied. "No words needed. And we can't believe it either. But that's how long God had destined him to live on this earth. I pray for you all to live long and be safe."

As our call came to an end, I felt like I had become a child again talking to her: the little boy hurt and crying while the kind aunt consoles him. That moment passed. Something, however, changed then so that I'll learn from my dreams that followed. Every time I slept, at night or for a few hours in the day, I had a dream in which I saw myself as a kid again.

In one of the dreams, spanning several long sequences, I saw that I was outdoors with other teams and the key cast of *Airwolf*, a show I loved in my childhood days. I saw that my brother and I were kids again and were having pictures of us taken with Jan Michael Vincent, the show's lead actor, by the combat helicopter, Airwolf. In another dream, I saw myself as a child sitting by a closet and looking at my clothes, wondering which ones to pick to wear. My mom appeared in the door and I asked her what I should wear. She gave me that you'll-never-learn look and told me to pick a certain shirt and trousers. In the next one, I saw myself and other kids taking some usual household items (shoes, books, boxes etc) and making a little garage sale with the belief that it'd make us rich since people would buy them thinking these were precious antiques.

What happened with my cousin's death that unlocked the child in me so that I started seeing myself as a child every time I slept and had a dream? Maybe a difficult or unacceptable news like my cousin's death triggered the child self of me to take over so that I could escape the pain of being an adult and look to a grownup—an authority figure—to console me while I just do my child-life things and free my mind from an adult's role—the painful one. I don't know. What I do know is that I was a kid again—locked into a state of childhood in my dreams, a leap back in time where I am not mourning and feeling helpless, but just enjoying my little innocent adventures.

That One Time

How many of them disappeared beneath the soil? I've lost count. They were all put in shrouds whenever their time came so those still breathing and walking could see them one last time before they went inside the earth. I was never there for that last look at any of them—including my father. I was always away, forever on the outside. They know I'm that guy—the one who loves keeping to himself, and hates gatherings. They have long stopped expecting me at any wake, no matter who goes. They know I won't act out the post-mortal rituals of respect that the person lying with closed eyes is paid by them. My lonesomeness has become a valid excuse for my absence from the last goodbye scene. Yet there was that one single time, one unavoidable last goodbye I had to say without running away.

That summer evening in 1999, when mom and siblings were away, I sat with a sinking heart by my 11-year-old friend. He was dying. The vet in the town's rundown animal hospital had recommended an oral medication to mix in his water. He said if my dog made it through the night, he'd have a second chance. So I sat by him on the ground, and when he moved in his silent suffering to another spot, I took his water bowl with him to make sure the water was in his reach whenever he got thirsty. The kaolin powder mixed in his water was his lifeline that he was counting on. Every time he drank a little from his bowl, I called his name—Kaloo—and caressed his salt-and-pepper fur. He would look at me and blink meekly as if acknowledging my presence. Yes, he knew I was there. And we both knew that night it was me, him, and death. In a moment, death would take him along with my hope that he'd make it through the night. I'd break down like never before as I see him becoming still after his last labored breaths while my hand gently rubbed his tummy. I could not save him. I did do for him, though, what no one else would—stay with him in his final moments, something I've never done for anyone.

The Game Begins

When the clayey carpet of the roof is not muddy with rain, I am carried up there in the pocket of a twelve-year-old boy who strolls back and forth across the roof. As he takes me out of his pocket, the town's green, hilly extremities lie bare before us. Just a ladder up from the bounds of his small house, its walls and people, my friend carries his notebook, a pen, and me—just what he needs for playing a game that he loves. It starts when I fly up and return to his hands.

Over a dozen players are in line today—characters from his favorite TV shows, some with names as he saw them on screen and others with names twisted by his imagination, for fun. All these names are penned down in the left column, the date neatly placed in the top right corner of the page. The players include men, women, and children. Who wins today? My friend doesn't know; the players don't know; even I don't know, though it's my flight and landing that will decide the winner. The sun lights the scene, filling the air with warmth. Parrots and mynas are popping out of their nests on that big, old *chinar*, sprawling out of the mosque next to the house. The birds love the morning, the sun, chirping and hopping joyously on the branches. Our game has a perfect setting. I can almost hear the heartbeat of my friend.

Suddenly I hear voices coming from the house—voices that my friend hates, words shot around like shrapnel in the air. Images of angry people with red faces and eyes bulging out of their sockets appear on the clear, sunny film of still air. His loved ones are angry again. The inhabitants of his house shoot venom from their tongues when they flare up, many a time over trifles.

"What you looking at?" someone yells down in the house. He knows who is saying what and how; so do I. We recognize all their voices, their tones, the relative bluntness of the bad words fired at one another. Our game is about to start. But the people down the ladder have started theirs earlier. They won't stop soon, as my friend and I know. No worries, though, since our players are ready to take over now.

My friend balances me on his thumb, and is ready to flip me up in the air, and set me free. The voices from the house get louder. The boy starts the commentary for our game: "All ready to go and the audience cheering already to see their favorite stars in action. Let's see who of the first two players gets the first point; it's two points for Jeeni, for heads, or two points for Makepeace, if we get tails..." A four-lettered word of abuse reaches us from the house. My friend's heart sinks. It's about time. He tosses me up in the air. Our audiences cheer like never before. The game begins.

Tick of the Clock

Pictures have something magical about them. Holding printed photographs of people dear to you—family, friends, and pets—gives us some kind of special power. It's like they are literally in your hands and you can carry them in your pockets. Perhaps it's for that reason I always had a feeling of unease about carrying photos. Looking at those still faces felt like eating food that has no taste or listening to music without melody. In a way, it's despotic—possessing a form of yourself or others devoid of life. You can destroy these lifeless figures whenever you liked. You own them. Tyrannical!

Not so with seeing yourself in something that doesn't show you others but only you. Countless times have I seen the charm of mirrors. Every time I stood before it, the view of myself, the sensation of *I* looking at *me* became more addictive. Perhaps it's the coronation of my ego when the view before me is *me* and the universe means *I*. This chance at supremacy doesn't come without strings. A three-letter word undoes the ego's pride and privilege that is at work through the mirror: age. Every tick of the clock moves the *me* away from pleasure, and closer to fear.

Then comes the time when we have to work on ourselves before rushing to the mirror, hoping to look better than the previous time. Dying hair, putting stuff on face, replacing the natural with artificial in the mouth, and every other little fix to win the visual argument against the mirror—the same glossy sheet that lovingly fed the *I* is now heartlessly starving it.

My eye has seen different. It has fixed the looking glass, not on the wall, but one running in the soil. Countless drops forming an ever-shifting sheet don't entomb me, but make me and erase me endlessly, long as I look into the current. They put no wall behind me but the sky, the vastness of which transcends me. I feel being in the sky and in the water at the same time. The tick of the clock disappears in the music of time.

Trapped One-to-Nine

+ Math – zero, one, two, three… eight, nine, ten. Ten is so impure – a reworked face of two unique entities. All math past the count of one to nine is boring. Jugglery of numbers!

+ She is getting married. Her mother loves shopping, cars, gold, and talking about how she can afford all of these. She worships wealth. "At least a million, but likely more," I hear her talking about her shopping plans for her daughter's wedding. A million! But then the groom is going to buy at least as much gold for her. Marriage, a trade of numbers!

+ May twenty-six in the year two thousand and eleven, or 05/26/2011—the worst numbers on calendar in Hangu's history. They say at least 30 people died, and kept counting. Rising number of dead bodies dug from beneath the rubble. They are counting numbers. A family friend's brother is missing. He got out of his house ten minutes before the blast. Never came back. Later they'll learn he was disfigured beyond identification, was taken and buried by someone else, mistaken for their missing son presumed dead. The mourners were not counting numbers. Just stuck in the time when it happened. But isn't time numbers?

✦ A little pup sitting outside the small shop in cold and wet weather. Hangu's people will call it beautiful weather; but the pup only looks at people with humble eyes of a starving beggar. He wants food. Customers at the shop don't notice. Does the shopkeeper? I buy the pup a snack of biscuits.

"Oh, does he eat biscuits?" the shopkeeper tries to look surprised. I am not answering it. I am counting the money in my hand. How many snacks can I afford to buy for the pup before I leave him to people who don't notice... and a shopkeeper who is not sure what hungry dogs will eat?

Tutoring My Little Secret

She is dead now and it's been years. But years before she died, I remember her pale white face on her bedridden body covered in blankets and lying in bed outside on the patio, to get some sun, close to where I sat at a table tutoring English to her niece. Fanny's aunt Sarah had a surgery, several months ago, for a deep spine injury after she accidently fell in her house. Surgery had saved her from complete paralysis so that she could even walk a little with support. When she did, pain showed on her face. Sleeplessness, lack of appetite, and unrelenting pain had reduced her to something looking like a skeleton.

It was natural for me to speak nicely and caringly to her. Each time I saw her, I'd ask how she was doing and how she felt. I always tried, somewhat helplessly, to convey that things were still not that bad with her, and there was hope. One day she asked me something I didn't quite expect.

It was a sunny morning in late February. Incessant rain had confined people to their rooms for nearly a week and we were all relieved to see the sun was still there. I had just started with the lesson when Fanny had to take a short break for some house chore. As she went out of sight, Aunt Sarah furtively looked at her old mother. Finding her asleep (and the fact the elderly lady was also hard of hearing), she addressed me.

"I wanted to say something if you could promise to keep it secret," she nearly whispered. The word *secret* kind of rang an alarm; I always disliked secrets. But I kept my countenance unshaken.

"Sure." I smiled and tried to look polite.

"I cannot bear this pain anymore." The look on her face and the tone of her voice corroborated what she said. "Will you bring me a little poison? Death will end my pain." Her words shot through me with a pang, leaving me dumbfounded.

"Oh no!" I could hear my voice ringing hollow like the beat from an empty drum. "Don't say so, please!" It was some challenge to make up something reasonable and helpful to speak there and then that would make her feel better.

"I've asked everyone in this house," she continued in her whispering tone. "No one is going to help me. What life is this that I have now? It's worse than death—all pain. Some shops in the Amber Market have this stuff. I thought you would…"

"Yes, but why think so?" I interrupted her. The moment that passed, while she spoke, was enough for my mind to come up with something to say.

"Hard times come in our lives," I said, "and they go away too. Please don't lose hope. With treatment and care, you will gradually get better. Don't think about death. Life will get better for you."

The lady listened with care and I felt happy to see my words seemingly working. I could see it on her face. She reminded me to keep the secret and I promised. On Fanny's return to the study table, I felt relieved. My trial was over and I felt exonerated.

As the winter gave way to spring, our tutoring table was shifted to another spot. I didn't see Aunt Sarah anymore but I did come to know of how she was doing as I would ask Fanny about her health condition. A week or so later, I learnt that she had started eating fruit, and asking for some snacks in a rare show of renewed appetite. It sounded like a sign of her return to life.

A couple of years later, I visited Fanny's house and came to know that Aunt Sarah had got much better and could now move about without support from her family. She also had put on a bit and was eating better. Feeling happy for her, I was finally willing to rid myself of this burden of her secret and so I did as I penned down the memory, but didn't share it until I learnt of her passing years later when I was in Oregon. It's in her memory that I decided to change my little secret to her story.

Welcoming Fake News

Sad news here, brother, Afaq Khan is not with us anymore. This line in the Skype chat with my brother in Pakistan shot through me like an arrow. My first cousin, my little brother figure, that intelligent and good boy who was about to graduate and become a young attorney, that Afaq we knew as a textbook example of a good guy, had died all of a sudden. Not 30 yet and dead! Could 2021 get any worse? It was June then and I hoped this was the last death in my loved ones for the year at least.

Talking to my grieving aunt, the next day, I broke down. Yes, I had prepared some words of comfort to say to her over her son's sudden death when I called, but it ended up the other way around—me sobbing and she trying to comfort me like she did when I was a kid and fell sick or was hurt.

A few weeks later, another Skype message from home informed that my 88-year-old aunt had passed away. It wasn't unexpected or a shock; the last time they showed her to me on a Skype call, she was alive in name only; despite the best care by my mom and siblings, her time was up. I mourned more the loss of my freedom to go home and see her before she left for good as I am stranded here in America waiting for the State Department to act on my extension-of-stay application while hoping that the so-called pandemic restrictions will be over before I am to board the flight back home. On every Skype call, she always asked me in her aging but very familiar voice, "When will you return?" Now she visits me in dreams, free to roam the universe while I am tethered to a piece of paper in waiting.

Some more deaths down the road, the joy of Christmas filled the air and December seemed to bring a more soothing end to a sore year. Then it happened again. Another Skype call from home across the ocean and my brother shoots me with another arrow dipped in grief. This time it's Jamal—our childhood friend and relative, son of my mom's friend at whose house I along with my brother and sister used to go for our Koran lessons. That was back in the '80s in my school days. After the lesson from Jamal's mom and grandma, all us kids played in their house, running around and making a lot of noise. The ladies were so laid back; they didn't mind at all while we knocked ourselves out before returning home around sunset. Jamal grew up to be a good and responsible young man and despite me not seeing him often, my family kept in touch with him and others all along. They told me he collapsed in his house last evening and died soon after being rushed to the hospital. Apparently it was an unexpected heart attack.

I talked to my mom, who was mourning Jamal's passing—him being a nephew figure for her. *How does a young guy in his 30s just collapse and die?* My disbelief was soon flooded by grief and I returned to my room after the call.

So Jamal is no more—much younger than me, actually my sister's age, who is the youngest of us siblings. I am supposed to believe that my childhood friend is no more, just like my cousin. I don't want to though. I am tired of all these news of deaths and destruction coming from people that I trust. I wish these were all fake news, the same fake news that I don't care about much and don't let them get to my peace. If only these bad news were fake news!

When Your Screen Broke Down

When you first entered your room that winter evening with the Danish university's acceptance letter in your hand, you didn't know how to bottle up your excitement. Growing up in that small Pakistani town, you had dreamt of flying to the world you had seen on your TV screen in that small room with a roof made of clay and thatch. It dripped water in the rainy season and your father didn't earn enough to build you a house like that of many other kids in your school. But that didn't stop you from dreaming, even long after your childhood. Finally, after growing up with your dream of the developed, beautiful west, you had a paper in your hand—the purple form for visa application that possibly could turn the dream into your world.

You did see, though, the requirements for visa application at the embassy. The purple form welcoming your admission also told you about the five thousand dollars to show in your name in a bank in Denmark. Inside, you knew something then; but you chose not to pay any attention to it; let nothing get in the way of this beautiful feeling of success. You knew you had been so good to them all—those people who call you their loved one. You were there for them; you ran errands for them when they needed it; you tutored their kids, most of them for free; you accompanied them to the hospital when they were sick, for you felt their pain; and you mediated when their attitudes cross-fired. *Why wouldn't they help you?* How senseless would it be to even think of them shying away from giving you your dream?

See, your problem was that you sometimes asked very wrong questions. This one too was wrong outright—why they *wouldn't* help you. Was it your fear that stopped you from asking yourself why they *would* help you? You trusted them and assumed they trusted you, even with money. Well, it was about time you start living off that screen where the Good Samaritans get the good they do back as a gift when they needed it. Now was your time to see, learn, and remember.

So how did you like what you witnessed—the frowns on people's faces when you asked with a forced smile about a *small* loan that you'd return in a few months? Was it good to hear whispers behind your back in your house—voices saying you were naïve and awkward asking for money? Who did you like better—those who made the most well-crafted excuses and politely showed you the door, or those who couldn't refuse outright but made sure they restrain their help to a counter offer where you wished they had just turned your request down? You must remember your good friend's words, "If nobody in your family is helping you, what reasons others have to do it when they hardly know you?" Cruel, yet true, and very worthy of remembering.

So my dear fellow, in a matter of months, when you finally returned to your room again that late spring evening, you held that purple form in your hand, as you were to throw it inside the closet with the Danish Embassy's rejection letter asking you to show the required amount of funds in your name. It's amazing that on that evening, you knew very well how to quell your anguish. You did learn. You were always good at learning.

Windy Day

On a windy afternoon, dozens of kids are running all about the ground of an elementary school in the small town of Hangu in Pakistan's northwest. I see and hear them laughing, some shouting in excitement, playing tag. Some are just running a race from one end of the ground to the other, and then back again.

My feet join them and my beat dances to the unseen rhythm of ecstasy in the air. The air caresses the moving bodies of the children who now know that they have an indefinite period of time during which the teachers are in what they know as "meeting". I have heard of it too; it sounds like the teachers sit together and talk about something, probably us. But do we care at this moment?

There is a war on the ground. Two or more small armies have armed themselves with fallen twigs, some with longer branches, whose leaves sway like a green wave of water in the air as warring groups of the little soldiers chase each other, their hair and tunics flying around in wind. There is no blood in this war, but laughter and ecstasy, pure happiness.

My eyes see an overcast sky. *Why is it not raining?* I wonder for a moment. Then I start running again with the kids, feeling myself light as a leaf happily detached from its branch.

Long after the wind has stopped, the grounds are silent, and the train of time has left the school behind by decades, the laughter of the children, their waving hair and tunics, and the bloodless war, all rest safely in the peaceful quarters of memory. Those children with the knowledge of having free time never knew that one day, when they are in different bodies and their thinking cooked hard in the oven of convention, they would not be able to run again except in panic; they would fear going out wherever there is a crowd as they would never be able to tell who, where, and when will be stricken dead with shrapnel as someone with explosives strapped to their chest blows themselves off in the crowd.

I look at the sky now when it's overcast. I don't think about rain anymore. I just look at the sky because I don't want to look at the grounds. I don't want to see any redness. I cannot tell if the bloodless sky can help the ground where the scene of play and ecstasy has been replaced by funerals, by crying mothers and grownup kids armed not with twigs but guns and rockets; by boots thudding all around, creating a rhythm that causes one to freeze and hide. I do see military helicopters in the air but they are far below the sky. My eyes stare at the sky way above them; the clear sky where the scene of our play remains intact. Kids are running and playing there; mothers are cooking for their families; fathers are out for work; teachers are in a meeting. I reach for the doves, and they welcome me to fly with them.

About the Author

Hailing from the town of Hangu in Pakistan, Ernest Dempsey (Karim Khan) grew up in love with reading and writing. He is a writer and editor with multiple American and International publications. He has published five books and numerous articles, essays, poems, stories, reviews, and interviews. His first screenplay ended as a finalist in the Southeast Regional Film Festival 2020 and he is looking forward to adapting it into a novel while he makes short films for his film company Twin Paws Productions. Dempsey travels between America and Pakistan and maintains a vegetarian lifestyle. He runs a conservative-leaning blog *Word Matters!* at www.ernestdempsey.com and has launched his new book review site Book Corner at www.bookcorner.us.

Fun Fact: For his pen name, Dempsey is frequently confused with TN-based American author Ernest Dempsey, who is the author of the bestselling Sean Wyatt series of books.

Running is natural--an act combining freedom of motion and personal energy to take one's body and spirit out of the "normal" mode of movement. We run early in our lives, starting in childhood. Nobody needs to teach it to us. Even before we are able to muster the strength and attain the balance for running with our bodies, our spirit is long familiar with running. There truly is something special about running.

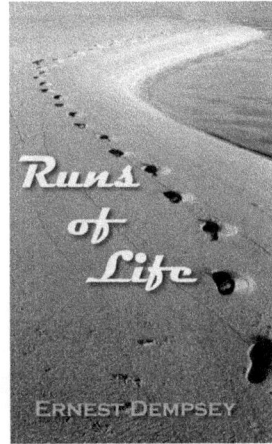

The themed poems in this publication come mainly from personal memories of running--out of simple play and childhood fun time, at times for safety, or even in dreams. I loved running; still love it though now I don't get many "calls" for speeding up my feet and setting my pace to that level of energy. But I do run, body and soul.

"Ernest Dempsey's dear little book on running is full of surprises. His earnestness about running both delights and transforms into potent metaphor.... just not the ones you might expect. This is a sweet and generous heart... one that runs into darkness and manages to bring back joy."

-- Elizabeth Knight, Writing and Literature Instructor, Portland Community College

"Not everyone remembers the joys of running the way that Ernest Dempsey has done in this little book. My favorite poem is 'Racing Heart.' Kudos to Ernest."

-- RD Armstrong, poet, publisher and dog about town

Learn more at www.ErnestDempsey.com
Modern History Press www.ModernHistoryPress.com

The Blue Fairy
and other tales of transcendence

Ernest Dempsey

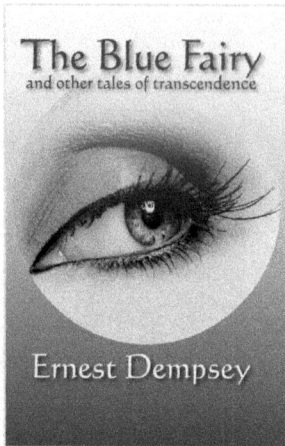

A thought-provoking excursion to life's last breath

Ernest Dempsey's second collection of short stories *The Blue Fairy* takes a subject that has been dreaded for centuries – 'Death'. It is one of the few works of fiction, which neither treats the subject as the 'D word' by bringing in fantasies of afterlife nor compromises the solemnity by trying to evaporate the reality of death in humor. Instead, Dempsey explores the many sides to the subject that make the final departure a meaningful reality of existence. Inspired mostly by real life experiences, Dempsey's *The Blue Fairy* ingeniously integrates dying with living. It is a book for the soul.

"There is something about the somberness of his search for moral principles that reminds me of Victorian poets such as Tennyson, Bronte, Kipling, and Hardy writing in the 19th century. Bringing these themes into 21st century views is an interesting task." —Janet Grace Riehl, Village Wisdom

"Following clearly in the footsteps of Rod Serling or his distant predecessor, Edgar Allan Poe, comes a fresh new voice in world fiction. Ernest Dempsey conveys the freight of emotion with a twist of irony in his first collection of short stories which address the tender lines between life and death." —Victor R. Volkman, host of Authors Access

Learn more at www.ErnestDempsey.com
Modern History Press www.ModernHistoryPress.com